Shall We Dance?

DANCE TEAM

by Candice Ransom

FOCUS
READERS

CHAPTER 1

READY, SET, DANCE!

It's halftime at the football game. The crowd goes quiet. Onto the field marches the dance team!

There are two types of dance teams. **Kickline** dance teams are noted for their high kicks.

Dance teams are popular at high school sporting events.

 A dance team performs in a competition.

Each kick is performed in **unison**.
Jazz dance teams mostly use jazz
dance **techniques**. Sometimes
a dance team will perform both
styles. Either way, dance teams
know how to entertain a crowd.

Dance teams grew from other activities. Cheerleading teams, drill teams, and pep squads all entertain fans at school games. The first cheerleaders yelled chants at football games. Drill teams march in patterns. Pep squads lead cheers, often using **pom-poms**.

DANCE TIP

Dancing requires flexibility. Always warm and stretch your muscles before a class or performance.

 Dancers try out for the Kilgore College Rangerettes.

Dance teams share features with those activities. The main difference is that dance teams dance.

In 1929, the first dancing pep squad performed in Texas. Then came the Rangerettes in 1940. The all-girl team danced and kicked across the Kilgore College football field in Texas. Other schools also formed dance teams. In 1968, the first dance team **competition** was held in California. Today, dance teams **compete** all over the world.

DANCE TIP

Dance teams perform to entertain. Make sure you smile and let the crowd know you're having a good time.

CHAPTER 2

FANCY FEET

Flexible clothes are important for dance teams. Dancers usually practice in leggings. These tight pants are easy to move in. Having the right dancing shoes is also key. Sometimes tennis shoes work well.

Dancers aim to perform their moves at the same time.

However, both kickline and jazz dance teams can wear slip-on jazz dance shoes.

The real fun comes at showtime. Team members wear matching uniforms. Jazz dance team members might wear glittery costumes with short skirts. Kickline dance teams might wear shorts or tights and a fancy top.

Both groups usually perform in slip-on jazz dance shoes or character shoes. Character shoes

 **Different teams wear different types of shoes.**

have high heels. They also have

straps across the feet.

CHAPTER 3

TURN AND KICK!

Dancing is fun, and that should show in dance team performances. This is called **showmanship**. But great dancers also must have technical skills. Dance teams combine steps from other styles.

Showmanship helps draw fans into a performance.

These styles include jazz dance, modern dance, and even ballet. Teams also break into **formations** such as a V.

Dancers are always moving. They work together as a group. This shows during pirouettes. Those are complete turns done on one foot.

DANCE TIP

When you dance, lift your chin and look straight ahead. Don't look at the floor or your feet.

 **A dancer practices a pirouette.**

Each member of the dance team turns at the same time. The audience watches the entire team, not a single dancer.

Kickline teams kick their legs above their waists. They often move across the floor while they kick. To kick high, step forward on your left foot and kick your right leg.

DANCE TIP

Keep your body straight and tall when you do high kicks.

 The Radio City Rockettes are known for their kicklines.

Next, step forward on your right foot, then your left foot, and again on your right foot. Now up goes your left leg. Your toe should be pointed. Your kicking leg should be straight. High kicks take lots of practice.

FAN KICK

Both jazz and kickline dance teams perform fan kicks. You can practice these at home.

1. To do a right kick, brush out with your right foot. Point your right toes toward the left corner of the room.

2. Kick your right leg upward. It should go toward the left corner of the room.

3. Swing your right leg in a half-circle. The motion should look like the shape of a fan. Your toes end pointed toward the right corner of the room.

4. Brush your feet back together and step down on your right foot.

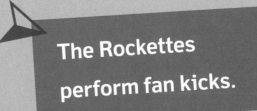

The Rockettes perform fan kicks.

CHAPTER 4

DANCE TEAM DREAMS

Dance teams borrow movements from other dance styles. That's why dance team members often take classes in styles such as jazz, modern dance, and ballet. Some even take gymnastics lessons.

College dancers perform at a basketball game.

Routines might require floor splits or **cartwheels**. Classes help dancers learn these techniques.

The summer is an important time for dance teams. Sometimes dancers go to camps. They work on their skills there. They also learn new routines.

DANCE TIP

Never wear your dance shoes on the street. Rough sidewalks can scratch the smooth leather soles.

> **Dance teams can help inspire school spirit.**

The fun really begins in the fall. That's when school begins. Dance teams often perform at sporting events. Sometimes they perform in pep rallies, too.

Dance teams also compete. Teams from different schools come together. Each team performs. Then judges score the performances.

The judges look at different things. They judge the difficulty of turns and jumps. They count the number of kicks in a kickline routine. They also judge if teams are performing as one. Whoever has the highest score wins. Some teams travel all over the United States to compete.

> **Dancers put on a show for the crowd.**

Dance team is about more than competition, though. It's about spending time with your friends. It's about performing in front of your classmates. And it's about having a great time dancing to fun music!

FOCUS ON
DANCE TEAM

Write your answers on a separate piece of paper.

1. Write a sentence that explains the main ideas of Chapter 4.

2. Would you rather be on a kickline dance team or a jazz dance team? Why?

3. What was the name of the first college dance team?
     A. Rockettes
     B. Rangerettes
     C. Majorettes

4. What might happen if a dance team member performed an incomplete pirouette?
     A. The audience would stare at her instead of the team.
     B. The audience would cheer on the solo performance.
     C. The dance team would be disqualified.

5. What does **techniques** mean in this book?
Routines might require floor splits or cartwheels.
*Classes help dancers learn these **techniques**.*
   A. games
   B. lessons
   C. skills

6. What does **borrow** mean in this book?
*Dance teams **borrow** movements from other*
dance styles. That's why dance team members
often take classes in styles such as jazz, modern
dance, and ballet.
   A. to give
   B. to copy
   C. to watch

Answer key on page 32.

GLOSSARY

cartwheels
Tumbling moves in which dancers do sideways handsprings.

compete
To work for a prize or reward against others.

competition
An event in which teams try to beat each other.

formations
Arrangements of people in groups.

kickline
A type of dance team in which dancers in a line kick at the same time.

pom-poms
Fluffy balls held by cheerleaders.

showmanship
The ability to perform in a theatrical way.

techniques
Skills used in physical movements, such as dance.

unison
At the same time.

TO LEARN MORE

BOOKS

Lusted, Marcia Amidon. *Cheer Tryouts and Training*. Minneapolis: ABDO, 2016.

Tieck, Sarah. *Dancing*. Minneapolis : ABDO, 2013.

Van der Linde, Laurel. *So, You Want to Be a Dancer? The Ultimate Guide to Exploring the Dance Industry*. New York: Aladdin, 2015.

NOTE TO EDUCATORS

Visit **www.focusreaders.com** to find lesson plans, activities, links, and other resources related to this title.

INDEX

B

ballet, 16, 23

C

camps, 24
cheerleading, 7
competitions, 9, 26–27

F

fan kicks, 20
football, 5, 7, 9

G

gymnastics, 23

H

high kicks, 5, 18–19

J

jazz dance, 6, 16, 23
jazz dance teams, 6,
     12, 20

K

kicklines, 5–6, 12, 18–19,
     20, 26
Kilgore College, 9

M

modern dance, 16, 23

P

pep rallies, 25
pirouettes, 16

R

Rangerettes, 9

S

shoes, 11–13, 24
stretching, 7

U

uniforms, 12

Answer Key: 1. Answers will vary; **2.** Answers will vary; **3.** B; **4.** A; **5.** C; **6.** B